better together*

*This book is best read together, grownup and kid.

 akidsco.com

a
kids
book
about

a kids book about

by Justin P. Flood & David Flood

a kids book about

Printed in the United States of America.

A Kids Book About books are available online: *akidsco.com*

To share your stories, ask questions, or inquire about bulk purchases (schools, libraries, and nonprofits), please use the following email address: *hello@akidsco.com*

ISBN: 978-1-951253-63-9

Designed by Duke Stebbins
Edited by Denise Morales Soto

Want to know more about David & Justin?
Follow David J. Flood, Youth Motivational Speaker
on Facebook or email at david@davidjflood.com

Interested in inviting David Flood to speak
at your school? Visit TopYouthSpeakers.com

For Mary and Sarah, we love you.

We'd also like to give a special thank you to:

Dr. Tim Hoss for your trust.

Tammie Topel for your inspiration.

Dr. Alan Sherr for your compassion.

Intro

Because we have a better understanding and acceptance of neurodiversity, more people receive an accurate and helpful diagnosis of autism spectrum disorder (ASD) every day. That may be your kid, you, or someone you know. The earlier we know that we all develop differently, the better for everyone.

We often don't fully understand the impact we have on those around us. We hope this book inspires everyone to pause before judging others. As you read, we encourage you and your kid to reflect on Justin's story and ask questions. Because understanding and empathy start there.

Hi,
my name is Justin.

This book is about autism,
and I am glad it found
its way into your hands.

Guess what?

I have autism...

why else would I write a book about autism?

I am writing this book
with my dad because
sometimes, I ask him for help.

(And sometimes, my dad
asks for my help too!)

I want to include my dad because we are like teammates, or best friends.

I hope you have a best friend, if you want one.

If you don't want one, that's good too.

Hi, I'm David,

better known as Justin's dad.

Here's the deal:
Justin is awesome.

And so are you!

I could just stop there because it's that simple.

But, I'd like to tell you something special...that's not why we wrote this book.

Hey, Justin, again.

I got it now, Dad, I'll tell them.

I want you to understand more about autism and people who might be just like me.

The full name is:

autism spectrum disorder (ASD).

There are lots of ways to say it, but for this book we're just going to say "autism."

I've asked my dad to help
with an explanation:

Autism is a neurodevelopmental difference in the brain.

Neurodevelopment means how your brain processes information and stimulus like movement, lights, and noises.

This means that the way someone's brain develops affects how they do things— which looks different

for everyone!

And this is why we say that autistic people are on a spectrum.

Look at this color wheel...

Do you see how it isn't
just one color?

It has hundreds and
hundreds of colors!

That's a spectrum!

Every shade is awesome,
just a little different.

Autistic people are like that too.

Hey, Justin, again.

One way to think about this is by understanding how people communicate.

I often have a lot of thoughts in my head and need to find a way to let them all out.

I talk a lot.

And some people I know who are autistic don't communicate using words, while others use just a few.

But language, communication, and talking are just one area you may notice differences in people with autism.

You might also notice we may:

move differently,
learn differently,
understand things differently,
ask for help differently,
pay attention differently,
make friends differently,
and interact with the world
around us differently.

Here's a few examples:

**I get very anxious
when I go up to someone and
try to make friends with them
because I'm afraid they
won't understand me.**

**Sometimes,
when I get really focused on
something and someone interrupts
me, it makes my head hurt
and I get angry.**

When I walk into a room, everything can sound **SO LOUD** and be **SUPER BRIGHT**.

When I look people in the eye, I feel like they're looking right through me, and that's scary!

How would that make *you* feel?

It sometimes seems like we're in our own world.

To give you a better idea of what it's like, here are some things I'm thinking right now, while I'm writing this book...

I hate the smell of shaving cream...

What was that!?

Is there a dog barking somewhere?

It's so loud.

Please be quiet!

There's always a connection for me, others just can't see it right away.

David, again.

I wish I could join Justin's world—
and I'll never stop trying.

I work to see the world
through his eyes, and that can
be really, really hard for me.

I've learned we can all be better at this when we let go of what we think we know and encourage the autistic person to share the thing they are interested in.

Lose yourself in their world.

Hey, it's Justin, again.

When I walk into a new place, I see everything there all at the same time.

All the time!

I see every color, sign, and person.

I hear every sound in every direction.

I feel the air against my skin and the tags in my clothes.

Kind of like this:

Where do I go? Wow, that is
buzzing. I need to get it. My d
listening. What's that song th
phone. That person's on their
and listen to my dad. There's
see that big potato. AHHHH, a
be my friends. What's that ove
That sign is really big. What i
from? The lights are really bri
Those people are talking reall
Where's my dad? I don't like h
so weird? What is it? I have to

! This tag itches. My phone is is talking to me. I'm not really playing? I have to answer my one. I can't stay off my phone rock in my shoe. Oops, didn't e! I wonder if those kids will here? I'm tired. It is soooo hot! at smell? Where is it coming My heart is beating really fast udly. Are they talking to me? that smells. Why does it smell the bathroom! RIGHT NOW!!

That's a lot, right?

It isn't always easy
to interact with others,
and this can sometimes
make me feel left out.

Here's an example...

I **REALLY** like going to the movies.*

When the movie is over, I'm really excited and I want to talk about it with other people!

*My dad and I have seen more than 100 movies!

So I'll walk right up to someone and ask what they thought about it.

A lot of times, they may look at me like I'm from outer space (cool!), ignore me, or walk away.

And that really hurts.

But...

I am resilient!

I'll keep trying to make connections with other people.

Just because things aren't always easy doesn't change that.

Autistic people are **AWESOME.**
It's true!

We are smart.
We are caring.
We are compassionate.
We are loving.
We are beautiful.

I like movies, video games, anime, and old cartoons.

I like chocolate, pizza, ice cream, burgers, and french fries.

I love trains, swimming, and golf with my dad.

I like meeting new people and getting to know them—even if they don't always understand me.

Just like anybody else.

David here.

I am not just David.
I am Justin Flood's dad.

I still don't always
understand Justin. :(

But, I'll never stop trying. :)

And I've learned that other people
will be your greatest teachers.

When you meet people who
are different from you,
you gain so much more
when *you* learn from *them*.

It might take more time to really understand autistic people, but that isn't bad.

It can be good because it slowwwwwwwwwwwwwwwwwwwwwwwwwww

wwwwwwwwwwwwwwws us down.

The world moves so fast, and we don't always take the time to slow down to a speed that works for everyone. We sometimes try to hurry others along to catch up with us.

Our job is to slow down and understand.

Remember all of those things
we talked about before?

When we celebrate the pace at which each of us moves, we build community.

And that's really, really,
really good.

Justin,
is there anything else
you'd like to say?

Nope. I gotta go to the movies, to an anime convention, to find a new Transformers figure, to...do it all!

Outro

It would be impossible to cover all the information about autism in one book— or even a hundred books. We have met, hugged, cried with, and listened to the stories of thousands of people. There is a saying in the autism community: if you've met one person with autism, guess what, you've met one person with autism! We are individuals. Yet on the inside, in our hearts and souls, we're all so similar.

Your kids will no doubt have a lot of questions after reading this book because autism is a huge subject.

We hope some of the ideas and examples we've shared help start a conversation with your kid about someone they know. We hope they get excited about understanding those around them a little better. We hope this book is one of the steps you take with them on their way to a life of dignity, respect, compassion, and true empathy for others. We hope you'll write to us and share your experiences. We love connecting with people and are glad that we met you here.

a kids book about MONEY
by Brian Watzer

kids book about BEING INCLUSIVE
by Ashton Mota & Rebekah Bruesehoff

kids about diversity
by Charlene Bauter

kids book about LEADErSHIP
by Orion Jean

kids book about IMM
by MJ Cala

a kids book about SAFETY
by Soraya Sutherlin, CEM
in partnership with JUDY

a kids book about CLIMATE CHANGE
by Zanagee Artis & Olivia Greenspan

a kids book about IMAGINATION
by LEVAR BURTON

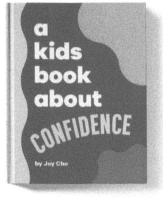
a kids book about CONFIDENCE
by Joy Cho

a kids book about

kids book about ANXIETY
by Szabo
Mind Happy Faces

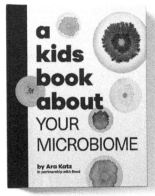
a kids book about YOUR MICROBIOME
by Ara Katz
in partnership with Seed

a kids book about racism
by Jelani Memory

a kids book about DISABILITIES
by Kristine Napper

a kids bo ab bon
by KYLE

a kids book about DIVORCE
by Ashley Simpo

a kids book about cancer
by Dr. Kelsie Storm & Sarah Porter

a kids book about BEING TRANSGENDER
by Gia Parr
in partnership with The GenderCool Project

a kids book about DEPRESSION
by Kileah McIlvain

kids book about ame

a kids book about THE TULSA